Searching For Home

Searching For Home

Poems

Robert Pack

SL/.NT

B O O K S

SEARCHING FOR HOME
Poems

Slant Books
P.O. Box 60295
Seattle, WA 98160

www.slantbooks.org

Cataloguing-in-Publication data:

Names: Pack, Robert.

Title: Searching for home : poems / Robert Pack.

Description: Seattle, WA: Slant Books, 2023

Identifiers: ISBN 978-1-63982-148-8 (hardcover) | ISBN 978-1-63982-147-1 (paperback) | ISBN 978-1-63982-149-5 (ebook)

Subjects: LCSH: American poetry--21st century | American poetry--Jewish authors | Science--Poetry | Nature--Poetry

Contents

THE BUTTERFLY AND THE SUN

Do you remember that our son
Was asked in kindergarten class
"What's very bright and comes out every day?"
Perhaps our son thought that
The question was intended as a trick
Because it seemed so obvious.
The answer that he gave
Was, "It is a butterfly."
His teacher said that he was wrong,
That the right answer is the sun,
And told us that he is not ready for first grade.
"A butterfly also is correct,"
We pleaded on our son's behalf,
"And has its own appeal, its charm,
And does evoke the image of the morning sun."

"Shakespeare's King Lear," I lectured the young teacher,
"Imagined the great joy he'd feel
When reunited with Cordelia,
His one trustworthy child.
Even in prison, so I believe,
They would be free from political intrigue.
Lear says, 'We'll laugh at gilded butterflies,'
Which might well represent for him
Transcendence in this world."
"Remember," I said, "in Greek myths
A butterfly is symbol for
The everlasting soul."

1

"In early fall," my wife chimed in,
"Thousands of Monarch butterflies
Gather in Canada to begin
Their long migration down to Mexico's
Central mountain villages,
Where tourists come to marvel
At the astounding spectacle.
(We need to make this pilgrimage ourselves.)
The butterflies ride the currents of the air
And navigate magnetically
According to the sun.
I don't know how their wings,
So delicate, survive the currents of the wind.
Their sunset orange color warns the birds,
'Beware, I may be poisonous to eat.'"

"Thanks, Dear," I teased my wife,
"For your reminding me
You graduated *summa* from
Your kindergarten class."

"But here is what I know about the sun:
In only half a dozen billion years,
It will use up its fuel, its hydrogen,
And enter its Red Giant phase.
Burning at three thousand K degrees,
It will expand, extinguishing all life on earth,
And thus fulfill its evolutionary fate,
At last becoming a White Dwarf.
And so, my dear, I move past you
As first in today's grown-up kindergarten class."

"White Dwarf, I fear, must have become by now
A term politically incorrect,
Doubly offensive to the sensitive
And now must be replaced
With something like James Joyce's 'Quark,'"
I hectored on, "which we now use to designate

An elemental particle.
We need to rename the White Dwarf
Something more entertaining,
Culturally acceptable,
Like Cosmic Has-Been or
Solar Schlemiel."

"Here is a mundane fact," my wife replied,
"About the Monarch butterfly
That seems to me more meaningful,
More empathetic, than just being factual:
Its most favorite place to perch
And rest its decorated wings
Is on a petal of a sunflower.
To start the day with a bright metaphor,
As even our son's teacher would agree,
Conveying peacefulness, evoking hope."

MY ODYSSEY

Sing now, my unrepentant sixth-grade Muse,
our adaptation of blind Homer's poem,
the fabulous outlandish *Odyssey*
which we performed for the entire school.
Our teacher Mr. Shore told us that
blind Homer had a special gift
for seeing contradictions in his characters.
The stage production we would mount, he said,
will emphasize fragility and chance,
the whimsy of the interfering gods
whose fates are held in doubt,
and we'll conclude with Odysseus
returning home after twenty years to his Penelope,
who has been faithful against all worldly odds.

Hooray! we shouted, jumping up and down,
laughing together, ready to set sail.
We would discuss why Odysseus
preferred Penelope, his aging wife,
over a goddess who could offer him
eternal youth. Does immortality
turn tedious? we wondered, is that
why Homer's deities' main activity is to amuse
themselves observing us, our follies and our suffering?

Empathy was the next big theme that we focused on.
Mr. Shore told us: "Heartfelt empathy
is the emotion to redeem mankind,

to free us from our self-indulgent lives."
So we decided that the episode
where tactical Odysseus pokes out
Cyclops's central single eye would test
our stretched capacity for feeling pain
on the behalf of someone different from us.

Cyclops imprisoned sailors in his cave
and planned to feast on them—Odysseus's crew—
but when the Cyclops slept that night,
Odysseus heated the sharp tip
of his trustworthy sword in Cyclops's fire,
then thrust it into dreaming Cyclops's eye.
Cyclops cried out in his tremendous voice:
"What is the name of the damn villain who
has blinded me?" Crafty Odysseus
replied, "It's me, world-famous Nobody."
The next day, when his neighbor asked who blinded him
Cyclops replied, "Nobody blinded me."
His neighbor taunted him, "If Nobody has blinded you,
what then is your complaint?" The gory scene
dissolves back in wild hilarity.

Our somber Mr. Shore decided that
we should attempt something original.
The Cyclops's scream will terrify the audience.
Don was the tallest member of our class
and thus assigned to play the Cyclops's part.
By nature Don was reticent, and so
he had to learn to howl for the high sake of art.

Richie, as the god Poseidon, will
perform the epilogue in which the sea god vows
revenge for his blind, mutilated son.
The sea will be Odysseus's nemesis
until he reaches home in Ithaca,
where his old nurse identifies him by his hunting scar.
With his well-aimed bow, he slaughters all

the meat-stuffed, cringing suitors—all except
the minstrel with his unforgetting harp.
Odysseus gives orders that
the household slaves be hanged
who had indulged in sex with suitors of Penelope;
we see their feet twitch in their agony.
What can one make of so much cruelty?
But we were children—we were
sixth graders, breathless with airy possibility.

I was assigned to play Odysseus.
I pasted flesh-colored adhesive strips
across Don's tightened eyes.
I cut a rubber ball in half,
fixed it where a center eye would be,
and painted a thick eyebrow over it;
and we were ready to begin the play.
The plot moved on to please the audience
until I smote the snoring Cyclops's single eye.
The rubber ball leapt from Don's head,
then bounced and wobbled crazily across the stage.

I don't know who first laughed out loud—
big Don, captured sailors, me,
or all of us together over frantic pleas by Mr. Shore
for us to persevere for Homer's sake.
Wave after cresting wave,
our laughter went rampaging through the auditorium,
reverberating off the paneled walls,
then out through swinging exit doors
into the street, into Laurel Park,
and then, uplifted by a dusty wind,
the laughter floated out beyond
the continent, beyond the legendary wine-dark sea.

Where is our sixth-grade laughter now?
Where does the bifurcated eyeball bounce
to find its final resting place?

Blind and immobile in my sunken chair,
I'm being read to by a female voice.
The slaughtered suitors' relatives unite to seek revenge.
They organize to march against Odysseus down by the sea
who with his father and his son are armed for battle.
Oncoming violence already shocks
the heavy air; the honey scent of blood
curdles their minds. Everything follows as it must.
Where there are men, there must be war—except
perhaps when a protective goddess intervenes
as militant Athena does
after Laertes kills a charging enemy.
Is intervention by a meddling god
the only way proliferating war can be
deflected and transformed to peace?

Is this the long-imagined homecoming—
Odysseus returning to the bed
that he had carved those twenty years ago?
Is this the flourish of the harpist's art?
Arpeggios to fill the emptiness?
Is this the laughter of oblivion?

SEARCHING FOR HOME

He instructed us in the mores of an ancient people,
which had known life in all its vicissitudes.

    —Eulogy for Phil Kaplan

1

And after the defeat of Germany,
after my father's early death,
while still attending Fieldston School,
I'd often take the train to Brooklyn where,
in a Jewish neighborhood,
including the Orthodox
dressed all in black with uncut beards,
lived my Uncle Phil, a fugitive from Russia.
Phil resided there with his exile wife,
a professional librarian,
and their two daughters, one a watercolorist
and one a concert pianist.
My Uncle Phil emphatically proclaimed
that art is how we rise above mortality.
    Back in Old Russia, Phil, an honored Rabbi,
led his own synagogue of worshippers
to whom he could preach his Reformist views,
his heartfelt jeremiads
condemning looting and the ravaging
of Jewish village shops and stores,

their merchandise of shawls and shirts,
of boots and overcoats.
But he came under scrutiny of the authorities.
He wondered what God had in mind
in so testing him,
and he was horrified to see
how some Jews turned against their being Jews
when threatened or coerced.

One night a stranger at his door
warned him he had to flee without delay
because the inquisitors were coming to arrest him.
While the moon still hid behind the clouds,
he disappeared, not to be seen again.
He fled into the Russian dark
with only his Bible and his fears.

2

Safe in remote America,
he revised his surname to Kaplan,
and Feivel became Phil.
Phil's family came one year later,
leaving behind their paintings, their candelabra,
and their heirloom silverware.

Phil was not able to regain
his rabbi status or find a role to play
in a new synagogue,
so to support his family,
he had to take a humbling job as salesman
in the cut-throat garment industry.

Right after we had morning tea,
he'd pack two suitcases with sample dresses,
but before he'd leave for work,
he'd give a sermon on a passage from the Bible:
"Father Abraham," he lectured me,
"would never sacrifice his son.
He knew in binding Isaac
he could outbluff God,

who then would have to back off
from the test of Abraham's obedience.
God wanted Abraham to be the one to seek
the Promised Land."
    Sadly, I'd watch Phil lift the suitcases
and disappear down the long flight of stairs.
    I had a dream the dresses all escaped
from their confining suitcases
and floated like ghosts out the open window
into the windy street.
Phil was amused when I retold my dream,
and his wife Pearl joined our laughter heartily.

3

I liked to visit overnight in Brooklyn
so I could schmooze with Phil
before he went grudgingly to work.
"Friendship, today, will be my sermon's theme," he said.
"Without friendship, as pragmatic Aristotle said,
life is not worth living;
it's nothing but an empty wind."
    Inspired, Phil leapt up from his chair,
went to his suitcase
and took out a sample dress.
He held it up, his arms outstretched,
and said to "her" in a falsetto voice:
"Whither thou goest, I go, too,
thy home shall be my home; thy God shall be my God."
Phil took "her" for a graceful spin,
and singing a melodic strain,
he circled the whole room
swaying till Pearl, in her pajamas, entered in
and took Phil's hand, swirled with him.
Phil's lithe daughter joined the dance,
and Grandma with a sprightly bounce
that I had never seen before.
They circled and they sang,

while I applauded to the pulsing beat.
I could have toasted them with French champagne;
I could have toasted them with chicken soup.
And yet the taste of other-worldly honey
lingered oh so lightly on my lips.

4

One rainy morning, I asked Phil,
"Why choose to be a Jew if one does not believe in God?"
"The choice," Phil rapidly replied,
"was made inside your mother's womb."
He paused, then said,
"Besides, we Jews do have the best jokes.
There are some ills and sorrows
for which laughter is the only cure.
The Jewish pessimist opines,
'Oy vey, things can't get any worse';
'Oh, yes, they can,' the Jewish optimist replies."
"Excruciating humor," Phil adjudicates,
"is almost capable of making what is
unendurable endurable."
      When God told the still childless Abraham
his progeny would be as numerous as stars,
skeptical Abraham laughed out loud,
and so did his wife Sarah, who
had given up all hope of motherhood.
Offended, God responded to her disbelief,
"What made you laugh?"
But, intimidated, she denied that she had laughed
in disrespectful incredulity.
And yet she lived to have a son
named Isaac, which means, "One who laughs."
"And add to that," Phil chortled, "Abraham,
when he reached ninety-nine years old,
was circumcised—and that, for sure,
defines what chutzpah is.
Abraham was cut out for leadership
for which we should feel gratitude."

5

When feeling mischievous,
Phil would recite for me
favorite passages from the Hebrew Bible
with his own augmentations
and irreverent embellishments,
so where the King James Bible read,
"God said let there be light
and there was light,"
Phil's gospel version was "Let E equal mc squared"
to make the point that from the start
our universe was indifferent to life,
and life was no more than an accident
or, at the most, a failed experiment.
Was not Einstein's own theology
a deity of fixed equations
and unalterable laws?

    And where the holy text condemns
our mother Eve for disobedience,
Phil as God praises her and declares:
"Let women make the big decisions
in all future stressed-out family affairs."
But Phil's self-entertainment ceases
when he thinks of Eve and Adam
banished from their garden home of fruited trees:
"God had to dress their nakedness,
as if they still were helpless children,
and God still was new to fatherhood."

    He'd say, "We're not ourselves in civil harmony
among the fallen nations of the world
when we rule anyone except ourselves.
And we can't count on the benevolence
of kings or tyrants or authorities
that flash a moment in the sun
to choose the path of holiness
that we were chosen to embrace."

6

"In my conflicted youth,"
said melancholy Phil by candlelight,
"I wanted to enroll
in newly founded Hebrew University
whose board of governors included
Albert Einstein, Sigmund Freud, and Martin Buber—each
the leading genius in his field."
    Einstein believed God was impersonal—
the sum of nature's laws—
the law of gravity,
the curvature of space,
the quantum leaps of light,
the ratio of mass to energy.
Amused, he would call the Hebrew God
Der Alter, as if he were a character
in a remembered fairy tale.
    Buber was Einstein's opposite.
His penetrating *I and Thou*
assumed that one's relationship to God
was personal, was intimate.
    Freud thought God was an illusion
that fulfilled the need to feel protected
and assuage the fear of death.
When he was asked
what is the goal of psychotherapy,
he quipped, "To replace neurotic misery
with ordinary unhappiness."
Grim, yes, but still funny, still curative.
Thanks, sympathetic Doctor Freud.
    "We've got to make ourselves at home
within the mind," Phil said,
"but also we have to make ourselves at home beneath the sun,
among the wavering of leaves.
Across an undulating meadow
and beyond a stream,
a land of memories,

where Abraham is buried in a cave,
where Moses found his conscience on a mountain top:
This is the land we now call Israel,
named after renamed Jacob who
wrestled with God throughout the whirling night,
and yet Jacob prevailed and received a blessing and,
with a dislocated hip,
limped off into the everlasting dawn."

7

Phil adored Theodor Herzl,
the founding spirit of an independent Jewish state.
"Jews need a place where they can go
in order to escape the massacres and the pogroms.
I'll never understand the hate,"
Phil said, "and fear the hate will never end,
that it is caused by our deep gift for suffering
and the haters' blind denial of their guilt."

8

Phil memorized poems from *The City of Slaughter*
by the Israeli poet Bialik,
and he could hum the gloomy melodies of *Boris Godunov*.
    He was appalled when Roosevelt refused
to let survivors of the Holocaust
disembark here in America,
but when in 1948
Harry Truman decided to approve statehood for Israel,
despite the bitter opposition from
his anti-Semitic cabinet,
Phil considered moving the whole family to Israel.
    The morning Phil informed me of the news
that Israel had officially declared itself a state,
he rose up from his chair
and did a little dance in front of me
and sang, "Hope is not dead.

The time has come for Feivel the Ferocious
to emigrate to Israel
and make the Promised Land our home,
where each long day begins in certainty,
the morning light reflects off angel wings,
approving breezes settle among orange trees,
and continuity is flow."
   We all decided then
to visit friends in Israel.
We toured the countryside
and stopped in order to inspect a kibbutz farm,
where we all overheard a boy, pointing his camera,
exclaim to his father, "Look there, Dad,
across the field I think that is a Jewish cow!"
   Phil knew he was too old to farm the land,
but maybe he could tend the olive trees
near where the ancient Roman soldiers,
two millennia ago, had leveled to the ground
the sacred temple of the Jews.
But who was he to judge the
Lord God's intents and purposes?

9

The early years of statehood were a trial
for Israeli citizens
who had to ration food—
an egg a week per family—
with crowded, heatless housing
for the waves of persecuted immigrants
who sought acceptance and relief.
   I still can picture Phil that year,
conducting seder for the family,
waving the matzo and the bitter herbs
to remind us of the hardships
that our ancestors endured
in the bare desert wilderness
when they escaped from servitude

in Egypt under the sadistic Pharaoh's tyranny.
How could he be the opposite, Phil mused out loud,
of the preceding Pharaoh
who befriended Joseph, Jacob's son,
and made him his estate executor
after he was sold into slavery
by his jealous brothers because
his father Jacob loved him the most?
In power, Joseph rescued Egypt
from the famine spreading through the land.
When Joseph's brothers came to Egypt,
seeking sufficient food supplies,
Joseph revealed his true identity,
and he forgave their former treachery.
Yes, sobbing he embraced them all.
    Then Phil concluded softly,
"That is how Joseph redeemed the primal eldest crime—
Cain's murdering of Abel in the field."
Phil gasped, and in a trembling distant voice,
whispered to us all, "The blessing and the curse
of brotherhood—that is the wound
that must be healed,
that is the everlasting wound."

10

In Genesis, our father Jacob
wrestled with an angel one interminable night,
and he miraculously survived.
As Phil explained to me,
Jacob was transformed and renamed Israel.
The new Jewish state, having endured prodigious obstacles,
the calumny of arrogant contempt, was named after him.
Embracing resembles wrestling, even strangling—
that is the fear Phil wanted to convey to me—
that love is not completely free of hate,
and self-approval is not far from self-contempt.
So Rosh Hashanah leads to Yom Kippur

with atonement for lust and greed
even when they take place only in the mind.
The Sabbath follows after labor, after strife.
After Jacob struggled through the night
to become the father of twelve tribes,
his hip came out of joint,
and Jacob limped on to his destiny.

    "Now is the time for me to choose
to make my legendary home," Phil said,
"where two millennia of promises
flower into bloom." I wondered then,
will Phil's ancestral wound be healed—
his longing to be father to a son?

11

When Israel's Ben Gurion began
negotiating with Germany's Kurt Adenauer
about reparations for the Holocaust,
Phil was outraged and shouted that
such money is contaminated filth.
The glass of water in his hand
exploded in his tightened grip.
"Some evil cannot be redeemed," he said,
and put his head down on his bloody hand.
He paused, looked up, and said,
"I know Israel's economy is bad:
machinery is needed for the farms,
a waterway is needed to irrigate the desert
and housing needed for the latest wave
of hungry immigrants.

    "Oh what a choice, my God, is this?" cried Phil.
"It is too late for me to be a citizen of Israel,
I am the past—the memory
of servitude, of promises delayed,
extermination that exceeds belief.
Today's Jews must be muscular and quick,
steady and resolute,

defiant and invincible."

Again, Phil put his head in his cupped hands,
and he began to sob. His sobs flowed forth
in pulsing intervals, and I,
in reverential harmony with his unfathomable grief,
I also sobbed and found relief for suffering
beyond what I could comprehend.

12

Having endured long years of workplace servitude,
Phil became the Moses of my mind—
the Moses rendered tangible in stone
by Michelangelo the Florentine
for all the citizens to see,
though Michelangelo depicted him
with horns like other Jews
as was believed in Europe at that time.
Yahweh, a god of war as once he was,
has now returned as lawgiver.
The tablet with the Ten Commandments
slips down from Moses's grasp
as he glares sideways in dismay,
appalled by what apostasy he sees—
the desecration of his holiness.

13

The quote that was a guide for him, Phil claimed,
was written by Talmudic sage Rabbi Hillel:
"Every man in the course of life
should have a helpmate and a child,
should build a house,
and plant a tree,
and also he should write a book."
Phil thought that some day
he would build a house in Israel,
and he still planned to write a book

in which, rescued from the river,
he eventually became a mighty king
who passes a decree
in which all marriages require
that couples have diverse identities:
Arabs would have to marry Jews,
and blacks would have to marry whites.

   After about three generations
everyone would be a little bit of everything.
People would pair and fall in love
simply because all humans need to feel
that they are loved. Love will then triumph
over hatred, its twin opposite.
Sin and hate will have no territory of their own
on which to arm themselves.
All wedding ceremonies will include
the planting of a tree,
and all attendees will be asked to wear
a Brooklyn Dodgers baseball cap,
the universal symbol
of good sportsmanship and loyal fans.
I see that Phil is pleased
with his political perceptiveness
and innovative policies,
and I am pleased that he is pleased.

14

After the UN's controversial vote
to recognize Israel as an independent state,
Phil thought that bearded Lincoln was
the Moses of America. Phil wondered whether
Lincoln's "malice toward none" Civil War-ending speech
could really break the chains of fratricidal animosity
and free us from what at our worst infernally we are.

   Phil's stuttering made his speech emphatic.
And I recall that Moses was a stutterer

who thought his brother Aaron was
more qualified than he
to face the reigning Pharaoh's wrath.
But at his lengthy farewell speech
to his assembled followers, Moses's voice
was fully in command:
"Choose life that thou mayst live."

15

The thought that vexed Phil most—
the base conundrum beating in his heart—
was that gray-bearded Yahweh was
the deity who first made ethical demands
of his true worshippers,
thereby creating conscience—
consciousness redoubled on itself—
so that no human mind could be at peace.
Phil wondered if the chosen Jews
could be blamed for dwelling
in the guilt of this morality.
"How many sun-scorched times
can the Temple in Jerusalem
be resurrected from the dust?"
Phil asked the emptiness.

16

Early this morning in a dream,
my Uncle Phil again returned to Brooklyn
where ghosts of warrior Maccabees
patrolled the cautious streets in pairs.
I see Phil climb the dusky stairs
without his suitcases,
sit at the oak table,
light the silver candelabra,
pour a cup of lemon tea.
He says, "I have returned to say 'Goodbye'

now that hope lies in the writing of a book
but this time I will get it right.
I won't ask if Jew-haters still believe
we drain the blood of Christian infants
for matzo at our seder meal
or plot to take control of the whole world.
They claim the Jews are guilty of
the crime of deicide.
No, thinking that way madness lies.
    "I only want you to remember that
we talked about beloved books,
about the planting of young aspen trees,
and that I loved you dearly
as if you were my son, my chosen son."

17

Reality and fiction intermixed
in Aunt Pearl's restless mind.
She loved the works of Dostoevsky
for their range of empathy:
Dmitri's passions, Ivan's intellect,
Alyosha's saintliness,
but couldn't reconcile his writer's art
with his abhorrent bigotry
and hatred for the Jews—
slander that one might hear in any bar
in any random neighborhood.
    When Adolf Eichmann was abducted
from his hiding place in Argentina
to Jerusalem to stand trial
for his crimes against humanity,
Pearl told me that Phil always had opposed
the penalty of death
as too severe for human frailty,
but in this case, she thought,
Phil would have found the spectacle quite bearable
of Eichmann dangling from a rope,

after five final spasms.

18

Phil still believed against grim nature's odds
that human creatures, by good will,
can transcend and can recreate themselves
in some places at some times
to care for strangers and the poor
and can accept the strains and the betrayals
of their competing relatives and friends,
forgive them, reconcile with them,
as cheated Esau did with Jacob,
and as Joseph reconciled with all his jealous brothers
when he wept and welcomed their return
in the abundant country of his heart.
    Israel's inclusive Law of Return,
Phil fervently believed,
was without recorded precedent
in all the history of politics.
Passed shortly after Israel
became a sanctioned state,
the law invited Jews throughout the world
to emigrate to Israel where, on arrival,
they'd be citizens with all their rights and privileges.
No longer disenfranchised and despised,
they then would have a home—
they would be welcome there.
    For those who choose to make their home elsewhere,
who find identity in work, position, or in wealth,
let Israel evoke the murmuring of bees,
like angel wings, around the orange blossoms in the wind,
let that remain the Zion of their minds.

19

My Uncle Phil did not live long enough
to learn of the great miracle:
the six-day military victory
of Israeli forces in the 1967 war.
The large Egyptian air force was destroyed.
The Golan Heights were captured and could now protect
the vulnerable villages below.
    After Phil's death, his wife Pearl visited
her friends in Israel and prayed beside the Wailing Wall
that Israel would not need prayer to survive.
People spoke Hebrew, kept the Sabbath faithfully,
and they atoned on Yom Kippur.
Before she left for home,
in loving memory of Phil,
Pearl planted two spruce trees.
Above her head an ancient hoopoe bird flew by,
his crest of tufted orange feathers
blazing in the morning sun.
Then she returned to America,
perhaps because her younger sister,
my grieving mother,
who wondered whether Jews
believed in Paradise,
feared another war in Israel was sure to come.

20

When Pearl was lying in the hospital
dying of leukemia,
the blood transfusion needle
in her outstretched skinny arm,
she took my hand and said
that Phil detested violence
but would have certainly rejoiced
at the Israeli victory in the war
and praised the workings of the Lord

despite his two millennium delay.
She drowsed off, then she said
that Keats was just a lovesick boy
in Italy, away from home,
far from beloved Fanny Brawne.
This world, despite its nightingales,
was never home for Keats.
And then Pearl whispered, "Pushkin"—
her last words to me—
"I loved him when I went to school.
I think that I was happy then."

21

Israel's Iron Dome defense
intercepts about ninety percent
of thousands of rockets launched
by Hamas terrorists within
the borders of the Gaza Strip.
Yet many get through and land randomly
among the wakened citizens.
That is how probabilities
express themselves.
Numbers exist in some Platonic realm
as absolutes even before
Big Bang created time and space
about fourteen billion years ago.
The citizens are jolted from their sleep
and scurry amid infuriating flames
to reach their shelters in the blazing night.
The dreaming children, half asleep,
are clutching their stuffed animals.
    Across the generating sea,
here in solid America,
the land of mergers, savings, and securities,
we cannot hide our own original identity
as tested Abraham's inheritors,
and I can hear Aunt Pearl repeat the words

of anguished Golda Meir: "We won't have peace until
the Arabs love their children more than they hate us."
      This may well be the long-expected date
on which all human life on earth
comes to its inevitable end.
Knowing our own nature
means that we also understand
our repeating visions of an apocalypse
as seen from the beginning of recorded time.
To know our nature is to know our fate—
our self-destruction that will bring about
our human end whether by flood or fire
or torrid radiation from a bomb
released by rebel Lucifer's command:
let there be energy
equal to mass times the squared speed of light.
Life's awareness of itself as life
will disappear into oblivion.
And what then happens to the past?
Does even having been cease to have been,
without regret? without cherishing?
      O, Phil, O uncle father Phil,
is it enough that I remember you?

22

Since Israel's founding, almost three million trees
have been planted in the hills and barren places,
where now their roots are watered by irrigation,
recalling the miracle of Moses
who summoned water from a rock
by tapping it with his commanding staff.
      Prime Minister Ben Gurion's
half-comic paradox,
"In Israel, to be a realist,
one must believe in miracles,"
expresses the contingency of faith,
the extremity of hope and of desire,

like Abraham's dread bargaining with God,
the chutzpah of his setting forth
to seek the Promised Land.

23

I can imagine Uncle Phil,
reclined beneath a tree,
reading Maimonides's *A Guide for the Perplexed*
by spectral moonlight.
Abraham, our ancient father,
floats down, sits by Phil, and says,
"The stars are yours if you can number them."
So Phil begins by pointing
at each one he can distinguish from the next,
but soon he drowses off as he imagines
that he's back in Brooklyn
where his wife Pearl awaits him on the Sabbath,
pours two steaming cups of lemon tea,
looks deeply in his searching eyes,
and one by one she lights the seven candles
of the silver candelabra in the dawn.

THE RIVER

Drifting along the smooth flowing river,
A melody by Mozart murmuring on my lips,
We watched the riverbank for browsing deer
And otters on their muddy slide.
But I'm not sure I can recall
Who paddled with me in the bow,
Her sunlit hair aglow.
I did not know where this smooth river ends,
Or what awaits us past the blue horizon's haze.

A rainbow trout arced in the air before us,
And still another arced behind.
Water globes dripped from my paddle
And caught the dazzle from the sun.
The river flowed on at its own designated speed.

She turned around to warn me that a rock
Protruded from the water up ahead.
The slant light of the sun blazed on her face,
And it obscured her features:
All that I saw was fear and disbelief,
The downturn of her mouth,
The disengagement of her sunken eyes.

MIND

. . . it follows when the scrutinizing mind
asks if it's free to choose and thus begin,
or if it cannot know itself, is blind
with groping thoughts: salvation, grace, and sin.

It follows that a solitary star
outleaps its orbit, unpredictable.
The mind is what it is, is what we are.
The mind swirls empty; then the mind whirls full.

Again mind follows its own following,
choosing its earliest necessity.
It sings the song that its ancestors sing,
again, again, determined to be free.

Fading, forlorn, on angel wings again—
it flows out—up—up and away and then . . .

TALKING TURKEY

A proud, plump turkey visits in our yard.
My wife takes him a bowl of sunflower seed.
Their voices mingle, and I listen hard—
I cannot tell her greeting from his need.

I think she's thinking what I'd think,
When sweetly seen flesh can be beautiful—
His wattle is a trembling reddish pink;
A white spot glows above the noble skull.

I stare through frosted glass to watch my wife.
The turkey stands secure in turkey space,
His body certain in its present life.
I see my wife stare, searching for my face.

What makes him so adventurous, so free?
I cannot love myself without her loving me.

PAIN

I know that you're in pain, and I would share
your suffering if sharing could assuage
what you are given to endure—the bare
wordless unmediated body's rage.

But I'm imprisoned by my helplessness,
my single sullen solitary life.
My mind is a surmise, an anguished guess.
My mouth is just a spoon, my teeth a knife.

Where is the history of suffering?
Without a story, no identity.
Without a mourner, there's no one to sing
that anybody walked here by the sea

Or, forlorn in the woods, in search of me,
in search of me, my dear, in search of me.

SURVIVAL SONNET

I'm ninety-three, I'm blind, you speak of hope.
My children live mute distances away.
I search for consolation, and I grope
For light—light unreplaceable for day.

Do you know me? I'm Bob, a palindrome.
You see me coming when you see me gone.
And home is now the memory of home.
I am the vanishing you fix upon.

You say I can beat time by beating time.
You say I can out-hum the humming bee,
And bring back mellow summer with a rhyme,
And float a fallen leaf back to its tree.

I call to you for better or for worse.
I am becomes iamb—long live rhymed verse.

SELF-DECEPTION

"You are my only love," was what I said.
I thought those words were what she wished to hear.
Where had the current of our stories led?
Uncertainty was what kept me sincere.

Was I truly the author of my vow?
Were her intentions visible that day?
Was I the same man then as I am now?
The rising wind blows fallen Time away.

I think that it was raining on that night,
And maybe rain affected my dark mood.
My eager promises did not sound right.
Though we embraced, it felt like solitude.

Which urgent I is I? Who wants to know?
Like water inside water, my thoughts flow.

OY VEY

Oy Vey! The students are addicted to
Their mesmerizing phones, and all they fear
Is others may not think the way they do;
They disagree, *Oy vey iz mir.*

I write this oy vey poem, though it is late,
For those whom my inheritors admire,
Not those revisionists who love to hate,
Whose greed for opposition never tires.

This oy vey poem is offered with a shrug.
How much can irony make bearable?
Franz Kafka found redemption in a bug.
Europa found divine romance is bull.

Can this new generation be the worst?
Oy Vey! As curser, am I also cursed?

WHO'S LISTENING?

Can hope suffice? The virtuous are not
Rewarded after death. The violent
Do not face fiery punishment for what
Distress in life they caused the innocent.

Deception and betrayal rule the day.
And what, oh empty wind, can now be done?
Conflicted love drives harmony away.
The voiceless wind is only wind for everyone.

No angels choir among the swaying trees—
Just emptiness inside of emptiness.
No happy ever-after dream can ease
Our waking yearning for forgetfulness.

Promethean blind hope for everyone,
Can we find comfort in oblivion?

DOGGEREL SONNET

Kevin, our youngest son, was six years old
When blue-eyed Peaches joined our family.
Free-spirited, obstreperous and bold,
Rambunctious Peaches in my memory

Tussles with yelping Kevin in the swirling snow.
Peaches chases after him like Achilles
Chasing Hector back at ancient Troy. Round they go
Among snow-laden, swaying hemlock trees.

Peaches leaps up in a tremendous burst
And snatches Kevin's woolen hat away.
She tosses it up in the air. She's first
To catch the hat as it descends that day.

Kevin pursues her for better or for worse.
Laughter erupts throughout the universe.

RABBI FINKELSTEIN'S THANK YOU PRAYER

"Does Yahweh enjoy a joke?" I repeat
To scholar/rabbi Louis Finkelstein,
Who suffered from arthritis of the feet.
What did God make of pain? Can blue turn green?

The body dreams sweet summertime will last.
How can it know that it is not a soul?
Laughter elapses fading to the past:
A hole within a hole within a hole.

Unless his rabbi wit can set him free,
Employing old Talmudic reasoning,
From aging body's mirthless misery
To let the liberated spirit sing.

"Thanks, God. Now I can die without a frown
From bottom up instead of from top down."

MOSES'S VISION OF HIS GOD

A stutterer, I did not want to be
The one confronting Pharaoh on his throne.
"Who shall I tell the Pharaoh ordered me
To order him, just me alone?"

"I thrive beyond all Nature, yet I am
Author of all human history.
I made the lion and the trembling lamb,
And, Moses, I chose you to speak for me.

"I am that I am. Tell him I am demands
You let his people go, yes, everyone,
To cross the wilderness of desert sands,
And not lay bricks in fierce Egyptian sun."

"Through me, the Pharaoh's daughter would defeat
Her brutal father's lust for mastery.
Why do the same atrocities repeat?
Will freedom truly make the people free?"

"You may be quite astonished yet to hear
That many unredeeming centuries from now
Another doubting Moses will appear
To save Black slaves who groan behind a plow,

"Or gather cotton in the scorching sun
As if desiring to return to when
Chaos contended with Creation
Desiring now to triumph once again.

"I needed a caretaker who is true—
Noah's inheritor. The Hebrew word for ark
Also means basket, the one that saved you
From infant drowning in the cursed Nile's dark."

LEAVING FOR MARS

1.

Nineteen-thirty-eight. I'm nine years old.
My father, mother, little sister, and I
Are sitting in the living room,
Our dinner plates settled on our laps,
Listening to the radio: Edgar Bergen
And his iconoclastic puppet Charlie,
With his high hat and his monocle.
How easy to forget the two are really one.
Suddenly, a voice announces Martians
Have invaded Earth, obliterating every
Defense that tries to stop their takeover.
Wild panic breaks out everywhere.
The president comes on to say stay calm.
My sister bursts into tears. And then
My mother: "Maybe that's the Lord God's way
Of wiping out all evil from the Earth."
I ask my father, "Why do the Martians
Want to go to war with us? What did we do
To injure them?" "Maybe they think they have
To strike first," the words stumble out.
And then a voice coming on the radio to say
The invasion is just a fiction. The author must not
Have thought his words would cause such
Widespread panic, that people were not so gullible.
Later he apologized. With fake humility.

2.

Three years later, the Nazis invaded Poland
And Czechoslovakia. In 1940, it was Holland,
Belgium, Denmark, and then France,
Whose Maginot Defense Line failed to hold.
My father spread a map of Europe
On a table top above a sheet of cork so we
Could stick in colored pins to mark the progress
Of the war, both advances and retreats.

Still, Europe seemed so far away and so unreal,
It seemed like I was playing *Battleship*.
But when the Germans surged eastward
Toward Stalingrad, I thought, for the first time,
That maybe we would lose the war, that England
Would be invaded, America bombed.
And soon another vision will appear to fill
The vault of history: in concentration camps,
Naked, emaciated figures marching single file
Through iron doors to meet their doom.

3.

For the first time, the deaths of innocents
Outnumbered those of soldiers.
Technology enlarged the realms of hate.
But was this believable? And did we actually
Use an atom bomb to win the war against Japan?
And why did the two Koreas fail to unify as one?
How is it we retreated from the napalmed jungles
Of Vietnam, baffled, shamed, humiliated?
Or that my own countrymen abandoned
Women and children, our loyal friends
In Afghanistan? Incredible, no? But there it is.

4.

Artemis, our newest spaceship, blasts off
To gather information to prepare for our journey
To Mars, some eighty million miles away, a trip
That will take roughly three-quarters of a year.
The ship will be enormous, the old Ark redesigned
To carry enough of us to start a pilgrim colony.
The Martian landscape contains water
And minerals and a carbon dioxide atmosphere
That can be converted into oxygen.
It has two moons—Phobos and Deimos—
Those warrior sons of mighty Mars,
Whose names signify panic and fear.
From Mars, the sunset's a white disk
Surrounded by a hazy blue that turns to red.
How beautiful and austere its stony deserts,
Its canyons and mountains thrusting up into the sky.
Gifted with reason and inventiveness,
Having survived the tides of aching emptiness
And created sympathy from grief, given
This second chance, will peace at last be possible?

BY THE SEA ON YOM KIPPUR

In May 1939, the United States turned away the luxury liner
MS St. Louis, aboard which were over 900 Jewish asylum
seekers in flight from Hitler's Germany. The ship was forced
to return to Europe. Two hundred and fifty of the passengers
would later be killed by the Nazis.

What violence have I, has everyone,
Still to atone for
On this gray Yom Kippur?
The first spilled blood that groaned out from the earth
And hovered in the air? We hear it still.

Walking along an empty beach,
A gust of sandy wind and fractured shells stinging my face,
I heard a clash of a high frothing wave
Reverberate upon the shore as if
An ancient shofar's notes
Thundered outside the walls of Jericho.

I wondered if there's something inside each of us
That causes war, as if
There's meaning of my own
I needed now to be atoning for
With no one listening and no one
With the power to forgive.

Maybe I've lived too automatically
As an American, overfed,
Protected warmly through the night,
With only a few hundred years of history
To take to heart and memorize,
Not as a persecuted Jew, despised,
Accused of killing God's beloved only son,
Accused of draining Christian infant blood
To fortify Jewish unleavened bread.
With an origin so deep
We Jews cannot be sure
What this most primal cause demands of us.
And so I must atone
For not knowing how
I must atone.

     Another foaming wave uncurls
And smashes hard upon the shore
As if across desert sand.
I see a hooded soldier's head lift up
Behind the barricading dunes,
A rifle butt beside his ear.
I see the hatred in his eyes.
Or is this hate projected from my eyes?
Or mine projected from his eyes,
Returning back to some vague primal curse?

     And counter to my somber mood,
I speculate: If all Israeli citizens
Dressed like David when he danced
Before the Lord in linen ephod cloths
Would Arab enemies be blocked
From shooting them in the besotted streets?
Would all the air be filled with laughter and applause
As if a comedy had rounded to a close
And everybody could go home again?

Another wave lifts up and crashes on the rippled shore,
And I can hear across the sea
A ram's horn bleat a universal welcoming.
I see a grove of olive trees,
Each olive like a candle flame.
Beneath the tree there rests a cornucopia
Spilling out nuts, and figs, and dates, and grapes,
All shimmering in liquid light.
A rabbi in his flowing robes
Whose voice I almost recognize,
Gentle and low, whispers to me:
"A portion of your field
Must remain unharvested by you
In order for the poor to harvest
with the labor of their hands."

A swirl of sandy wind
Circles my head and stings my eyes.
I do not know where my heart's journey yet may lead
Or to what home I may return.
I only know, in Sabbath inwardness,
Today is Yom Kippur in luminous rebuilt Jerusalem.
That it is Yom Kippur, atonement day,
In clamorous and darkening America.

FEEDING THE DEER

Just seven years ago,
Here in northwest Montana
Below the spreading Mission Mountain range
Where we live, the deer were plentiful.

In summertime, they came and snoozed,
Grazed and sprawled upon our lawn at ease,
Certain that they were safe with us nearby.
When winter came, and snow piled higher
Than I could recall, I began to worry
That the deer would starve;
I bought a bag of pellet deer feed.
I put on my thick wool hat and fur-lined boots
And went out to a smooth-topped boulder there to wait
With deer food in my open hand
To see if any deer would come, and, yes,
To my delight, head down and cautiously,
A doe arrived, and took some needed food
From my gloved hand, stepped back, and stared at me.
She turned around and scampered back into the woods.

Next day, same time, same spot,
I went back to the boulder, filled my hand with food,
And stretched it out into the wilderness.
To my delight, two deer approached,
And touching head to head,
They ate together from my hand.
A chill seized me, so I went inside
To warm myself beside the fire.

Next day, the third, I went back to the boulder seat.
To my delight, it was not long
Before three does arrived.
They rubbed and pushed against each other,
Yet each ate her fair share,
Then disappeared into the forest shade
As wind stirred in the thrumming trees,
While curled dry leaves scattered across the loosened snow.

On the fourth day, when I sat down,
Almost instantly before my startled eyes,
More than a dozen stomping deer
Collided in the agitated snow.
I do not know how many deer I fed
That swirling day, but soon my bag of pellet food
Was down to only crumbled bits.

I realized I could not feed them all.
I looked up into emptiness
And heard the roused wind
Wail a threnody among the swaying trees—
The tamaracks, the spruce, the aspen,
And ponderosa pines
That sometimes live four hundred years—
Four hundred years without remorse.

OTTERS BELLYFLOPPING

We needed to escape, to get away,
And so we hauled our green canoe out of the barn
And pushed off from the wooden dock
Into the stream and took the tide.
We felt the water's pulse, the surge,
And paddled out into the river's flow.
A rainbow trout leapt into the air and made an arc
As if suspended in the light.

We drifted on, and there on the near bank
Two deer emerged from the thick underbrush
And dipped their tawny heads to drink,
Then paused to watch our passing there.
Across the stream on the far side,
A heron lifted from the reeds,
Stretching its vast wings toward the light.

We glided on, and there on the east bank
An open space revealed a muddy slope
Where otters skidded down into the foaming stream.
One by one, they climbed back up
Illuminated in the noonday sun,
Repeating their descent, their vanishing,
Into the water's swirling dark.

I do not know how long ago it was
When we two drifted in our green canoe,
But I can picture still the rainbow trout,

Its arc suspended in the air,
And I still see the two deer drinking
At the low lapping water's edge.
Lifting their heads, they watched, unperturbed,
Our easy passing with the flow.

"Look there," I said, "there in the space
Beside the underbrush
A family of otters
Is bellyflopping down a muddy slope
Into the churning waters of the stream.
That is," I continued, "an image palpable enough
To make the abstract concept
Of enduring happiness believable
Even here in this fleeting world."

And when we grew too old
To ride out safely in the stream,
We sold the green canoe
To a young couple down from Canada.
It was not long before they wrote to say
The green canoe had been destroyed
When it crashed on a jutting rock above a waterfall.

And somehow, suddenly,
My resurrecting thoughts flew back
To that illuminated day
Of otters bellyflopping, steering
With their sturdy webbed feet
Down the mud slope into the stream,
Repeating their delight, as if
their sun-drenched pleasure would not end.

"Yes, I remember," my wife said:
"It was as if the wind had opened up a space
Within the tangled underbrush
Where otters could construct a slide
Into the rushing stream below,

And then climb up again, again,
Repeating their descent into the stream—
Contented to be what they are,
Happy to be otters, and I was
Happy in their happiness."

TAUNTING REVERSED

Our son attended a small country school
Where kids came mainly from farm families.
Each morning I would drive him to the school
Where his friends greeted him.
They'd merge together in a throng
Then run off like a swarm of bees.
One day I dropped him off in my red streamlined Saab,
And, totally to my appalled surprise,
His farm friends gathered in a crowd
When he jumped carefree from the car.
They chanted in rough unison:
Rich kid! Rich kid! Rich kid! He's a Rich kid!
Where had this hostile taunt come from so suddenly?
Was it instinctive? Was it inevitable?
The taunt continued through the week.
His teacher asked me if I wanted her
To intervene, but my son said
That he would handle this himself.
Next day, the teacher told me what she'd seen
And what my son had said
To all his astonished friends.
He put his hands upon his hips,
Puffed out his chest, and challenged them:
You'd be rich, too, if your dad
Got up early in the day
To write a book of poetry.

And so, Dear Readers, Classmates
Of the Universe, as you can see,
My couplet runneth over.
I strut my strophes in adversity.
Some poems arrive by lucky chance
And only need embellishment
By the sweet muse of offbeat memory,
Where kids' taunts will someday be
Transformed to richest poetry.

AT LAST

We know the world is coming to an end.
Although this is not what we tell our wives,
It's certain the time has come to send—
So that at least our epitaph survives—

A mighty capsule into outer space
With sample souvenirs of what we've done:
Our music and our poetry that grace
The discontented lives of everyone.

Now all that matters are the final days.
The sunset spreads out slowly on the lake;
A fish leaps from the silent water, stays
Suspended for an instant for my sake.

I'll wait for you to find me in the past
Where there is nothing more to lose—at last.

À LA DESCARTES

"I think, therefore I am," declared Descartes,
Convinced he had an everlasting soul
To soothe the sorrows of his mortal heart
Assuring him that Time would make him whole,

With Reason sovereign upon its throne,
And Passion not desiring to be free,
Subdued within the blood, within the bone,
Now ready to endure Eternity.

But you can find me here among the beasts,
Aroused by lust, driven by appetite,
Boldly advancing with unplanned retreats,
Believing what is palpably in sight.

With the snarl of a wolf, the bleat of a lamb,
Sometimes I think, therefore sometimes I am.

GLOCKENSPIEL

In Mozart's opera *The Magic Flute*,
A flighty bird catcher—Papageno
Is his name—desires a wife who's cute
And fertile, plump above and plump below.

He searches for her hotly through the land
Protected by his magic Glockenspiel,
And everyone attuned can understand
The noted feelings that he awaits to feel.

Is Papageno Mozart's alternate
And Papagena one more variant?
Is this how Mozart did himself create
With melody surpassing its intent?

Klinget, Glöckchen, klinget, Papagena sings
For all of us, for our transfiguring.

PLAYING MY SELF

1.

I walk along a brambled path beside a lake
surrounded by a mountain range. On an out-
stretched branch, I see a patch of thick
brown hair and know what has preceded me.
Exhausted, I sit down on a fallen tree
and gaze out at the lake. I drowse off
to waken to a large brown bear sitting
next to me. He yawns, and I yawn with him.
We watch white haze swirling from the lake.
We watch the golden tamaracks reflected
in the lake with its arched swans taking flight.
Then the lake returns to its sunset red.
Blown clouds dissolve as the swans
prolong their vanishing. Suddenly, the bear
lifts up, scratches his back upon a tree,
and disappears into the forest shade,
leaving me to scratch my own itching scalp.

A moose, dripping from the lake, approaches
and stares at me. His long jutting jaw resembles
FDR's, New York's governor when my father
was assemblyman. But what's left now of that
old New Deal? Where are the folks who peddled
apples in those melancholy city streets?
Or those who leapt from windows to their doom?

2.

I drifted off again, and when I woke, an angel
sat beside me on the fallen tree. "I have a message
from your mother," she whispered. "All she's ever
asked of you, she says, is that you do
your very best. That best will be the authentic
you, and to do that you will have to stay aware."

I rose up from the tree and hurried down
'til I reached a clearing in the woods
where a funeral was taking place. A
casket was waiting to be lowered in the earth.
In his white yarmulke and shawl, the bear
stood praying by the open grave, then blew
his ram's horn to welcome everyone.
On a marble headstone I could read the words:
"Here lies Bob Pack who never could retire,
he had so many ironies in the fire."

I was delighted that I got to hear
what my survivors had to say. Five
old friends chanted our high school
football cheer and praised me for my
Jewish jokes, their "oy" contained within
their joy. "He took delight in his egregious
puns. And, yes, he loved that animals breathe
the same air we breathe while the light lasts."
"Don't forget my modesty," I mumbled to myself.

My wife was there, holding the hand
of someone I barely recognized. "I recall,"
she said, "that summer he sang his favorite role—
Mozart's Papageno—at our town's festival
with Mozart's music on his lips, embellished
with his magic glockenspiel. Never was he
more joyously himself. Having endured
the torments of desire and the last temptations

of despair, he doubled down, with Papagena, contented and fulfilled."

QUINTESSENCE OF DARWIN

1. DARWIN'S TESTAMENT

When Darwin reached old age after
a lifelong malady that drained his strength
and caused him nausea that interfered
with innovative research on worms
or barnacles or climbing plants,
he'd ask his wife at evening by the fire
to read to him out loud from a worn book
he was assured concluded happily.
Surely there was sufficient suffering
in daily life even for those who felt
adversity can strengthen character,
thus giving purpose to what might appear
inscrutably evil, though such belief,
congenial to human pride, did not,
he knew, apply to animals who lack
consoling words to ease starvation or
the grip of a determined predator.
    Though evolution brought forth varied forms
most beautiful to contemplate—a process
Darwin described as having "grandeur,"
his awed sense of Nature's plenitude
was superseded by the evidence
of Nature's cruelty and waste
and then confirmed beyond remaining doubt
when his beloved Annie died of fever
that parental care could not abate

at only ten years old, without
an outcry of protest by her to shake
the smooth striation buried in the hills.
     And yet it brought him joy to understand
how natural selection could create
uncanny patterns and resemblances,
expressions of contentment or of fear,
on human faces everywhere
across the separating continents,
in children, and in chimpanzees.
     The shaded colorings of finches' wings,
the varied sizes of their beaks,
enabled Darwin to forget his gloom;
he took delight in adaptations like
a frog that's capable of climbing trees,
a fish that can change sexes if
a sudden mating opportunity
presents itself, a forest bird
that feigns it has a broken wing
in order to distract a stalking fox
from sniffing out its nest of naked chicks.
     How plants respond to stimuli
engaged his boundless curiosity,
so Darwin had his son Francis improvise
on his bassoon beside the close plant
domesticated in his care. I like
to think he heard it whispering its thanks.
All living things, he was convinced at heart,
composed one single seamless family
and shared a single origin.
     Darwin had solved the deepest mystery
of how new species could evolve without
the intervention of divinity,
and thus the mystery of humankind,
yet the enigma of his unique
identity as witness to our being here,
his joy, endurance, and his suffering,
remains elusive to our enquiry.

Perhaps his malady was caused
by some germ he contracted on
his youthful, five-year journey
in tropical South America
or in the unexplored Galapagos.
Or maybe he had violated some
inherent innocence of Nature with
forbidden knowledge symbolized
in the fatal apple scrutinized
in outcast Adam's reaching hand
whose consequences only could be
understood too late to remedy.

Is this the burden of his testament—
knowledge of how we've been created to
become the conscious creatures we now are,
desiring permanence, enthralled by change—
green shadings of transfigured green—
successfully surviving for a while?

2. GRIEVING FOR ANNIE

When we behold a wide turf-covered expanse, we should remember that its smoothness, on which so much of its beauty depends, is mainly due to the inequalities having been slowly leveled by worms.

—Charles Darwin

Prolific Darwin is remembered for
his ailments and his generosity
toward loyal friends, consideration for
his wife's lifelong religious faith,
devotion to his many children,
Annie in particular, who died
of fever at the age of ten.
    Darwin's commitment to the truth
of how Nature designed itself, based on
observation and analysis,
evidence, despite the consolation
offered by a Christian afterlife
that needed to be given up, provides
a model for the tolerant of stomach
and the unequivocal of heart.
    Darwin's great theory of selection and
descent—how creatures struggle to compete
since their supplies of food are limited—
is the most powerful idea ever
conceived by humankind because
of its explanatory scope and depth:

we all remain at heart what once we've been.
Species will flourish in their time,
become extinct when circumstances change,
and vanish never to return again—
a truth excruciating to accept.

   Darwin thought evolution had produced
"forms beautiful and wonderful."
The "war of Nature" was a process
he described as having "grandeur"
since increased complexity had led
in time to human consciousness,
society, and moral sentiments
like sympathy, benevolence, and trust.

   But Darwin's attitude about how
Nature operated to select the fit
kept darkening until, disburdening
himself of pent-up anguish, Darwin
wrote to Joseph Hooker, his good friend,
condemning Nature's works as "clumsy,
wasteful, blundering, and horrible";
no consolation for inevitable
conflict can be found except perhaps
through human care and tenderness,
the pleasure that we sometimes take
in bringing pleasure to someone we love
as little Annie surely did for him.
He wrote an elegy extolling her,
"It was delightful to behold her face,"
recording her last quaint and gracious words
as "I quite thank you" when he held
her head and offered her a final drink.

   And yet it's dubious that evolution
can account for such unselfishness
or tell him where to look for consolation
in a world where loss, unmerited
and indiscriminate, seems absolute
beyond repair or recompense.
Surviving Annie's stupefying death,

Darwin continued to be burdened by
the marble weight of mournfulness,
and yet he went on working since his work
allowed for self-forgetfulness
and granted him the patience to endure.

Twenty outreaching years after her death,
Darwin composed a book in praise of worms,
comparing them to gardeners who
"prepare the ground for seedlings of all kinds,"
depicting worms as cultivators—first
among the farmers of the earth.

Did Darwin find some consolation in
the laboring of lowly worms who plowed
the soil for ages immemorial
in knowledge of renewal through decay?
Could such relief suffice for him
and ease the ache of his undying grief?

3. PANEGYRIC FOR CHARLES DARWIN'S NOSE

for John Glendening

Before Captain FitzRoy began
his five-year journey on the *Beagle*
to explore the coast of South America,
he interviewed Charles Darwin whom
he thought to be God-fearing, pious,
and thus suitable to share his cabin
and to dine with him when he was not
exceedingly morose—although
he ended up by taking his own life.
    But FitzRoy didn't like the young man's nose,
believing that a man's true character
revealed itself according to
the contours of his face. Despite
his reservations, FitzRoy asked Darwin
to enlist as the ship's naturalist
to study new terrains, new habitats.
Despite his father's fervent hopes
that Charles would serve the holy church,
he gave his son consent to go.
    Consider, wide-eyed reader, this
incredible contingency! Had FitzRoy chosen
someone else because he didn't like
the twist of Darwin's nose—which showed,
so FitzRoy thought, a lack of energy—
the history of science might have followed
quite a different path in understanding
why we have emerged to be the creatures

that we are: cruel and competing,
struggling with others, and because,
as in the size of the finches' beaks,
we're also capable of sympathy,
struggling as well with our split selves.

   Just random chance, contingency,
something sublimely trivial—the shape
of Darwin's nose—that almost
but didn't quite sufficiently offend
FitzRoy's exquisite sensibility,
turned the fortuitous into our fate
to comprehend contingency itself,
which well might cause our warring species
to destroy itself or to survive perhaps
through some emergent self-control.

   Darwin's wife Emma married him for love,
not only to pass on her genes, although
she bore ten children: little Annie died
of fever when she was just ten years old;
another died of who knows what in infancy.
Emma, however, kept her faith and thought
that God created all the animals
as they are now six thousand years ago;
he fashioned humankind in His own image
but justly banished our first parents
from protected Eden when they disobeyed
his clear commands for self-restraint.
Emma believed that Jesus was
the needed savior of us all; it deeply
troubled her that Charles had doubts.

   So here's the nitty-gritty choice
that Darwin had to make: whether the world,
as he'd been brought up to assume,
was made by God, with moral laws to guide
our wayward impulses—or else
did we evolve through adaptation,
struggle, and raw randomness,
from variation, he so carefully observed,
with no hope of transcending death.

Contingency! Contingency is what we who
seek some consolation find for mere accident,
for suffering, for knowledge that
even species won't survive. Just understanding
is what Darwin's gloomy theory offers us:
blind variation and descent
wins the debate, but only by a nose,
and earns our admiration for his courage
to reject the soothing fables of the past.

And so I picture him and laugh out loud,
his awkward nose advancing into fame
and notoriety. O nose extravagant,
O nose unique, inquiring nose,
nose of discovery, of revelation
and astonishment, I offer praise to thee!
Enraptured connoisseur of beetles and
old tell-tale bones, Darwin, I see you still
astride a giant long-lived tortoise on
the rocky shore of the Galapagos,
your nose held high into the tropic light.

4. DARWIN'S BEETLE

With my new hip I'm able now to walk—
I am not finished yet—and so I hiked
out to the woods to test my stamina,
but, sad to say, I tired and had to rest.
As I sat down on a decaying log,
my hand descended on a beetle which
I placed upon my palm to contemplate
the bond I share with other living things.

    As a young man, Darwin would walk into
the countryside to seek rare beetles he
could add to his collection: one clear day
he came across two beetles, snatched them up,
and headed briskly home, pleased with himself,
a beetle in each hand, to mount them each
according to its color, size, or form.

    On his way back, eyes down, he spied still yet
another specimen not seen before
and hotly was compelled to capture it;
but since both hands were occupied, he put
one wildly squirming beetle in his mouth
to free a hand, but yuck! the beetle then
excreted something acrid on his tongue,
and Darwin had to spit it out; repulsed,
he dropped a beetle from his hand to clasp
his burning mouth, and he returned with just
one specimen as trophy for the day.

    That episode took place some years before
he sojourned forth to the Galapagos
where he collected untold multitudes

of specimens, of subtle variants,
finches that differed just according to
the sizes of their beaks. And there his first
great revelation of how things evolved
through struggle or eventually died out
began to take shape in his thoughts, although
he never did forget the day the angry
beetle fouled his tongue and thwarted him.

Imagining how Darwin felt—as if
it were my own experience—I taste
the panicked beetle's desperate excreta
Darwin spat out in disgust that day,
saving itself from its apparent fate
of being pinned to represent a blink
in nature's purposeless experiment
of hungry life competing with itself.

As I displayed the beetle in my palm
and I beheld its shimmering, I thought,
Ah well, Dear Helpmate, just compare
our troubles in this gated world
at home here dwelling where we are
ephemeral in sun, in rain,
with those of Darwin and his wife.
Emma, unwavering, believed
that Jesus was her savior and
assuredly would bring her up
to heaven when her days with earth
as home were over and complete.

The problem for her Christian faith
was Charles' theory about how
we human beings had evolved
entirely by Nature's laws, like universal gravity,
and not divine creation by
a loving God. Such new ideas
were blasphemous and without hope
and might well make impossible
admittance into Paradise.
The thought they'd spend the afterlife

apart, alone, tormented her.
Can Paradise without dear Charles
be Paradise as promised her?
Did God not fashion Eve to fill
the wound of Adam's loneliness?

    Charles thought that Nature can produce
new forms, designs most beautiful,
the wooing ornaments of birds,
the higher animals, and yet
the cruelty of natural
processes and phenomena,
famine, and bloody appetite,
and struggle went on without end.
"A Devil's Chapbook," he once wrote,
would list Nature's atrocities.

    Rapturous in boyhood, wholly
distracted and absorbed, Darwin
roamed meadows, hills, and fields to search
for beetles he could add to his collection's worldly treasury.
Beetle-questing I understand
and his comparing finches' beaks
far off in the Galapagos.
But what have I, a skeptic Jew,
to offer Emma—I who can't
contend with pissed-off Yahweh who
tells me (check out Leviticus) that I have fallen short of his
severe demand for holiness,
concern for all the desolate,
the unrequited and the poor.
As for the Ten Commandments, well,
not coveting for me is still
the very hardest to obey
because it's wholly in the mind.

    In the last year of his long life
of illness, disability
that still cannot be diagnosed,
and studying his "farmer" worms,
how they can cultivate the soil,

Darwin received a specimen
for his astute analysis:
a water beetle with his legs
caught in the grip of a grim clam.
But on arrival in the mail,
the beetle somehow freed itself,
though it was weakened and had lost
its vital animating strength.
Charles put it in a bottle with
some chopped up laurel leaves that oozed
a substance like an opiate
to soothe the beetle's suffering
and ease its speechless creature-way
to empty, everlasting death.

But here, my own Dear Helpmate pal,
the rosy apple of my eye,
temptress, cajoler, my spared rib—
here is a bright epiphany,
my gift to your forbearing heart.
Right here in the confounding dark,
picture the whole admissions board
for entry into Paradise
as bleary rabbi angels with their cloaks as wings,
their yarmulkes as shaded in dim candlelight.
All are Talmudic exegetes.
Unanimously, they agree
Charles Darwin should be granted a
full membership in Paradise
as his deserved award for his
wondrously magnanimous,
species-transcending empathy,
to be with beloved Emma up above,
where no doubt, I might safely add,
astonishing varieties
of beetles trippingly abound
amid the fields and tangled banks
to be collected and arranged,
neatly in rows, each one in place,

distinctive in its own design,
preserved for all eternity.

5. DARWIN'S WORMS

Charles Darwin's father wanted
his beetle-collecting son
to follow him in his medical profession,
but Charles applied for a position on the ship
the *Beagle* that was about to sail
along the coast of South America,
mapping the shoreline for the British government.
    Captain FitzRoy, a phrenologist,
believed one's character was revealed
by the bumps and contours of one's cranium;
so he examined Charles to see
if he was suitable to serve
as naturalist and a man
who could ease the solitary burden of command.
But the shape of Charles' nose concerned him because
it showed a lack of character,
so he almost turned him down.
Instead he signed Charles on for two years
that stretched out to five.
    Biology and theology would never be the same:
our special status as possessors of souls
was summoned into doubt.
But do only humans have souls?
Descartes and FitzRoy thought so.
The elephant, however, with its capacity for prolonged grief,
with its mourning for the dead,
might have a soulful aspect just as well.
Ah, yes, I like that thought, though thinking
is more likely to dispense or bring on gloom.

Brute mortal flesh is soulless except when
longing for a soul it can't possess
or when it is able to accept
abject, impersonal contingency.
    Perhaps thought caused Darwin's lifelong malady:
he suffered from chronic nausea and searing stomach pain
that nobody could diagnose—not then, not now.
Maybe it was Darwin's stark belief in his own blasphemy—
that no God had created humankind
and death was permanent—
that caused his sickness.
Studying his beetles and his barnacles,
the burrowing earthworms,
explorers of the underground,
helped him endure his evolutionary thoughts.
    Captain FitzRoy, a fundamentalist, rejected Darwin's theory.
On the Origin of Species appalled him:
FitzRoy believed the Genesis account of origins,
but his pious beliefs were not enough to save him.
Suicide lurked in his lineage,
the past was inescapable, and so
the day arrived when he,
FitzRoy, rebel against nature's primal law
and his Christian faith, slit his own throat.
    Appalled by the ghoulish atrocity,
remembering their days at sea, Darwin
contributed to a communal fund
to aid the forlorn widow in her grief.
Charles Darwin journeyed in his mind
to the volcanic Galapagos blazing in the tropic sun,
the mystery of finches' beaks—
some thick, some thin in bold variety—
the slow longevity of tortoises
and iguanas crouched on lava outcroppings.
    Darwin never ceased mourning for his daughter Annie,
doomed forever to remain ten years old.
He could not free himself from his own thoughts.
But where beneath the sun did Darwin learn

transcendent love?
Old age brought him more excruciating stomach pain,
more wrenching nausea,
except when contemplating living forms, like silent worms
that soften up the dirt, aerate the soil,
and cultivate the earth with nitrogen,
inheritance of bodily decay,
without which life would not be possible.
Darwin called them the world's first gardeners,
sounding a graceful note to mitigate
the groans of struggle and the clash of war,
the moans of famine and defeat, despite
the grandeur and the plenitude that fill
our mortal space recounted in
his *Origin of Species*, his
"Devil's Chapbook,"
his humankind-transforming book
that shudders deep within our bones.

DETERMINING EINSTEIN

"I am a deeply religious non-believer."
  —Albert Einstein

1. EINSTEIN'S LAST DAY

In the beginning, Einstein thought the speed of light
and the ubiquity of Time composed the mind
of Nature like a god whose might
was law with music as the soul of humankind.

He had a gift for friendship and felt bliss
performing Mozart on his violin.
He was more at home in that world than in this.
He summoned Newton—there to begin.

On his last waking day, he still would try
composing an equation that would be
successful in his wish to unify
his newfound law of relativity

with "quantum weirdness," as it was fondly called,
with randomness and probability.
Although determined, Einstein was appalled
by a god who traffics in uncertainty.

So what conclusion is this leading to?
Can we ask a deity to ease our suffering?
The "thou shalt" laws must suffice for me and you,
for every banished people's wandering.

We wanderers search for meaning in the mind,
our aching hearts go out to humankind.

2. EINSTEIN'S MARRIAGE

Einstein's first marriage, though begun ecstatically,
Turned into anger and to bitterness.
His genius had not known which self to be
And left his wife and sons in dire distress.

The early passion for his first wife was gone.
He needed someone much more motherly.
"My happiness," his new wife Else said, "does not depend upon
My understanding relativity."

Kindness he craved—kindness for everyone.
And I am able to imagine that
On a cold winter night, chilled to the bone,
Else might have left a dish of milk for Schrodinger's cat.

Suspended unseen between life and death,
The cat breathes the uncertainty of breath.

3. SPACED OUT ON TIME

Einstein loved the strict order of Nature's laws,
The sacred beauty of geometry.
And if there were sufficient evidence to cause
A change of views, he would generously agree.

Pragmatic Einstein knew with certainty
Theory must be confirmed by experiment.
Space can be altered by gravity,
And linear light is able to be bent.

To see light streaming from a distant star,
We need a full eclipse, we need the dark.
Self-questioning observers we are,
Elusive as a photon or a quark.

Einstein's prediction of the curving light,
Mercury's orbiting around the sun,
Would prove his theory either wrong or right—
Space would not be the same for everyone.

"If I am proven right, the Swiss will say
I'm Swiss. Germans will claim me as their own.
If I am proven wrong on judgment day,
Germans will claim I'm Jewish to the bone.

"Meanwhile, hate-driven war still rages free,
Hatred within and hatred without.
Where is Mozartian high harmony?
What is this inner hatred all about?"

Stranger, be kind to me in time, mindful and true,
And I'll will to be kind in time with you.

4. EINSTEIN FOR THE LEAGUE OF NATIONS

Einstein, despising national aggression,
requested Doctor Sigmund Freud give
his own perspective on violence—why men
think killing gives them greater vital potency to live.

They cling to an illusion, to a lie
of their survival, immortality,
that time will not run out—they will not die
and disappear forever, cease to be

without a body or a plot of trees,
a place to make a sacred home,
with identifying boundaries,
like paired rhymes resonating in a poem.

E = mc squared, Einstein well knew,
revealed we humans now could fabricate
an atom bomb that had grim power to
destroy us all with primal hate.

The cosmos is a fatally indifferent place,
with Einstein as a Zionist of space.

5. EINSTEIN ON PEACE

In 1938, a questionnaire
at upscale Princeton University
revealed the well-heeled students there
selected Hitler as the man to be

the most admired and the most esteemed,
ahead of Albert Einstein, number two,
a wary, worldly Zionist who dreamed
of universal peace yet also knew

the mystery of wrestling in the dark
as Jacob sought the mystery of light,
the conflagration from the spark,
the history of blood, the soul of sight.

And then came *Kristallnacht* in Germany,
the burning of synagogues and Jewish stores,
the cutting of throats in their sadistic glee,
civilian murders and civilian wars.

Albert Einstein, pacifist, would have to cease
believing that disarmament could bring us peace.

6. EINSTEIN AND FREE WILL

Free will exists if one is so inclined
to think that it exists. Einstein could see
that thinking is the glory of the mind
and the main cause of human misery.

Einstein well knew that gravity alone
determined the geometry of space,
a metaphor that we can call our own
and give our history a human face—

demonically human. As the First World War
broke out in Europe, Jewish scientists
were hated, banished, castigated for
just being what they are. Evil exists.

If choice is an illusion, who's responsible?
And what determines the design of Fate?
The moon is a sickle, then the moon is full.
There is a time for love; there is a time for hate.

He had not "overcome uncertainty"
and asked if freedom really could be free.

7. LOST AND FOUND

He left his Princeton office one fine day
and headed home. No longer living in Berlin,
he was confused, and he had lost his way.
Where was he still at heart a citizen?

He managed somehow to contact the Dean
to ask if he had Albert Einstein's home address.
He answered, not intending to be mean:
"We don't give information to the press."

And Einstein found himself remembering
the Nazi persecution of the Jews,
thug Hitler's fanatical murdering.
Einstein abandoned his pacifist views.

"Incredible! Can evil such as this be true?
My tormented thoughts are in a tempest whirled.
What can the biblical *Der Alter* do?
Does He play dice in a blaspheming world?

"Can we be free at home here in this universe?
Is thought a blessing, or is thought a curse?"

8. EINSTEIN'S PIPE

Hans reunited with his dad again
When immigrating to America.
He had two healthy sons—ages five and ten.
His scrawny, unattractive wife Frieda

Converted to the Christian Science Church.
Einstein, grinning, was overheard to snipe:
He also would be willing to convert
If he were free to keep his faithful pipe.

Hans's son was banished to his body's hell.
Aflame with hot diphtheria, he died.
Untimely death! Was it preventable?
The time for nothingness had then arrived.

And what was needed now was a little space—
A wooden rectangle two feet by three.
Silence had settled softly in its place.
Is consciousness of consciousness what makes thought free?

Remorse and sorrow are ephemeral.
The past endures just as the past.
Einstein's tormented mind is full
Of contradictions. Only equations last.

Einstein nuzzles his beloved pipe as if
It were the nipple of eternity.
Bodily pleasure is enough.
There's nothing further to desire or be.

Love and despair are inextricable.
Like waves and particles—bound by one law.
Einstein's grief was practically invisible.
His ashy pipe slipped down his loosened jaw.

Einstein believed that consolation must suffice,
Yet feared *Der Alter* did indeed play dice.

9. THE ATOM BOMB

When Einstein learned uranium can melt,
Knowing that mass can change to energy,
He wrote a warning letter to Roosevelt
Which said: "An atomic bomb is a possibility."

An atom bomb is deaf, and it is blind.
Is there a mortal cause worth fighting for?
The mind must overcome the hostile mind.
As long as men remain just men, there will be war.

After the conflagration in Japan,
TIME pictured Einstein as the father of the bomb
Whose $E = mc2$ revealed him as the man
Whose revelation caused the world such harm.

Einstein concurred with Hobbes's *Leviathan*
And felt most free when he removed his socks.
"In World War Three, we'll fight with bombs—that is the plan,
But World War Four will just be fought with rocks."

And Einstein realized this outcome was the worst—
Unless German scientists discovered the bomb first.

10. EINSTEIN'S LAST TRY

Einstein believed up to the very end:
Every discrete event must have a cause.
The Old One is neither parent nor a friend,
Does not play dice; he's obedient to laws.

Nature is what it was and that,
We know, is what makes science possible.
Shrunken face or grinning, Schrodinger's cat
Is either dead or fully sensible.

Soon after Hitler was made Chancellor,
Einstein departed for America
Never to return again. German no more,
His sense of self began to blur.

He'd never see his schizophrenic son.
Mileva, his first wife, also will die mad,
Repeating "No" and "No" and "No" to everyone
In her last days—immeasurably sad.

Is anyone to blame for this? Is he?
So then, is everybody innocent?
Is this the way the universe must be?
Is this Big Bang's original intent?

Our destiny, our being what we are,
The nuclear bomb ticks down as we
Destroy ourselves like an exploding star,
Annihilating all humanity.

I picture Einstein drifting in his boat,
Named *Tinef,* meaning junk, a Yiddish word,
Singing a Mozart aria, each note
Numbered now upon his lips, a nested bird.

An observer-dependent universe?
Must the observer then be self-aware?
Created by a god who does play dice?
Can the observer be a mouse, a bear?

His only absolute: the speed of light.
Is free will real? What makes compassion right?

11. *DER ALTER*'S LEGACY

Still, Einstein loved the biblical account:
A father god who got creation right
By balancing equations—numbers count—
Commencing with the words "Let there be light."

Reconciled son Hans arrived in time by plane to be
Beside his failing father who, when he awoke,
Quipped, "I should have studied more geometry,"
Atwinkle with the pleasure of his joke.

He'd written an arousing speech to be read
To celebrate Israel's anniversary,
Which was lying there composed beside his bed.
He hoped to bring peace in his own century.

"One single life is quite enough for me,
And Nature's laws are comprehensible—
That is their beauty and their mystery.
My Jewish soul is satisfied; my father heart is full.

"I don't believe in immortality;
What torment to eternally be young.
Law must be grounded in necessity."
His final words were in his mother tongue.

His bedside nurse did not know what they meant,
And so, by chance, his life's last words were spent.

Publisher's Note

Robert Pack passed away in June, 2023, soon after completing the final round of edits on the page proofs of this volume. The publisher would like to extend sincere gratitude to several individuals whose invaluable help made this book possible: John Glendening, John S. Hunt, Paul Mariani, Patricia Pack, and Jim Zanze.

This book was set in Baskerville URW. It was originally designed by John Baskerville in 1757.

This book was designed by Shannon Carter, Ian Creeger, and Gregory Wolfe. It was published in hardcover, paperback, and electronic formats by Slant Books, Seattle, Washington.

Cover photo: David McEachan, via Unsplash.